THE GREATEST GAMA

THE UNOFFICIAL STORY AND FACTS ABOUT INDIAS GREATEEST WRESTLER

Baksh A. Zubair

Baksh A. Zubair

GREATEST GAMA

INTRODUCATION

Gama Pehalwan was the epitome of a strongman; he never lost a fight in 50 years, performed hundreds of squats and pushups every day, and legend has it that he once fought off an entire crowd. When the mob realized who they were up against, they fled.

TABLE OF CONTENTS

<u>INTRODUCATION</u>

<u>CHAPTER ONE</u>

THE GREATEST

<u>CHAPTER TWO</u>

THE STONE LIFTED BY GAMA
WHAT YOU SHOULD KNOW ABOUT HIS DIET AND WORK OUT ROUTINE

<u>CHAPTER THREE</u>

HIS MYSTERIOUS DEATH
RELIGION AND FAMILY BACKGROUND OF GAMA PEHALWAN

TOUGHEST OPPONNENT

GAMAS FAMILY

GAMAS WIVES

CHAPTER ONE

THE GREATEST

Gama, whose real name is Ghulam Mohammad Baksh Butt, became an instant phenomenon in the county after drawing Rustam-e-Hind (Indian champion) Raheem Baksh Sultaniwala. Despite the odds being stacked against him, Gama fought a fair fight against the veteran wrestler. After all, Sultaniwala was seven feet tall, and a wrestler who was only 5'7" tall wasn't considered a contender.

Sultaniwala, on the other hand, was towards the end of his career and needed to find a way to draw after a tense struggle with a much more agile Gama. Gama's tenacity during the fight garnered him praise, and he was soon dubbed the Rustam-e-heir.

Gama's reputation grew as he was undefeated in his 52-year wrestling career, with opponents barely lasting a minute in front of him. And in London, the 110kg champion ruled supreme.

He defeated world champion Stanislaus Zbyszko, Frank Gotch, and Benjamin Roller on his way to the World Championship (Rustam-e-Zamana) title in 1910.

During his overseas trip, he defeated well-known players including Maurice Deriaz of Switzerland, Johann Lemm (the European Champion), and Jesse Peterson of the United States (World Champion).

Before retiring in 1952, he had an unblemished career.

Gama went undefeated for nearly a decade before retiring at the age of 74. With the exception of a few formidable opponents, he dominated the majority of his fight.

Sultaniwala, who pushed Gama for two hours in their first match, was one of the few wrestlers who the World Champion couldn't beat for a long time, and later admitted that the former Indian champion was the toughest opponent he had ever faced.

Gama, however, won the Rustam-e-Hind championship after a protracted battle after he returned from England.

During the 1947 partition rights in Lahore, he saved Hindu lives.

Gama won respect off the mat, too, when he rescued the lives of Hindus living on Mohni Road in Lahore, where he moved in

GREATEST GAMA

early 1947, just before India's independence and subsequent division.

Gama swore to save the community's lives with his life amid the increasing tensions of rioting and honored his word by holding rioters at bay from endangering the colony's occupants.

He then led them all to safety at the border as riots erupted, covering their meals for a week.

Kulsoom Nawaz (daughter of Hafiz Butt), Gama's granddaughter, was Pakistan's first lady three times after marrying former Prime Minister Nawaz Sharif in 1971.

Bruce Lee and Prince Charles both admired him.

Gama was known for his stringent diet and training regimens, and he was strong and muscular. He was said to do 5,000 squats and 3,000 pushups every day. Bruce Lee, a well-known martial artist and movie actor, borrowed some of Gama's skills as inspiration.

During the Prince of Wales' visit to India, Gama was also recognized for his bravery.

1200 kg stone lifted

GREATEST GAMA

Gama, who was in his early twenties and weighed roughly 100 kilograms, once pulled off the incredible feat of lifting a 1200 kilogram boulder at the Baroda Museum in Sayajibaug ahead of a competition in the city in 1902.

CHAPTER TWO

THE STONE LIFTED BY GAMA

Most modern weightlifters would huff and strain to lift a few hundred kg in professional competitions, despite years of training and exercises. However, in 1902, a young boy in his twenties stunned Barodians by lifting a stone weighing over 1,200 kg. Ghulam Mohammed alias Great Gama Pehalwan , a world-renowned figure, had lifted the stone from Nazarbaug Palace in Mandvi.

The stone, which is now kept at the Baroda Museum in Sayajibaug, stands two and a half feet tall and bears inscriptions. On December 23, 1902, Ghulam Mohammed, according to the text inscribed in it, raised the stone. When he accomplished the feat, Gama was in the then-Baroda state for a wrestling tournament.

He was the best wrestler in the country at the time and was undefeated until his death in 1960. "According to entry number 10-10 in the museum registry, the stone was added to the collection after 1912. Gama is reported to have lifted the stone upon his chest. We have kept the stone on exhibit outside the museum since it is historically significant "R D Parmar, the museum's director, stated. Gama, who was born in Amritsar in 1882, won the World Heavyweight Championship in 1910 after defeating renowned wrestlers in London.

After Maharaja Bhawani Singh of Datia, a princely ruler in Madhya Pradesh, became Gama's sponsor, he began wrestling at the age of ten and went through rigorous training.

Maharaja Sayajirao was a huge sports fan who used to organize a lot of competitions. Gama had come to town to compete in a wrestling match. He was a champion who couldn't find anyone who could compete with him. As a display of strength, he raised the stone and carried it for a short distance.

The fact that the museum authorities are having trouble moving the stone even with the support of 25 people demonstrates Gama's physical prowess. The stone had to be hauled inside the museum by 25 workers and a hydraulic machine.

CHAPTER THREE

WHAT YOU SHOULD KNOW ABOUT HIS DIET AND WORK OUT ROUTINE

- **The undefeated**

DURING HIS OUTSTANDING FIVE-DECADE CAREER, THE GREAT GAMA REMAINED UNBEATABLE.

- **Started Young**

AT THE AGE OF TEN, HE DID EACH DAY 500 LUNGES AND 500 PUSHUPS.

- **Defined Intense Workout**

Every day, he performed 5000 squats and 3000 pushups.

- **The Power Diet**

20 LITRES OF MILK, HALF KG OF PURE BUTTER, 4 KILOGRAMS OF FRUITS, AND LOTS OF YAKHNI WERE ALL PART OF HIS DIET WHEN HE WAS IN HIS PRIME.

- **SPECIAL DRINK**

MILK, SIX DESI CHICKENS, AND 500 GRAMS CRUSHED ALMOND PASTE MADE INTO TONIC DRINK

GREATEST GAMA

- **HIS SQUATS**

India's champion (Rustam-e-Hind) used to squat with a doughnut-shaped workout disc weighing 95 kilograms

- **Rare Achievements**

He once carried a stone weighing over 1200 kg at a wrestling competition in Baroda.

- **Inspiration to others**

Gama taught Bruce Lee 'The Cat Stretch,' which was a yoga-based version of push-ups.

- **The World Champion**

In 1927, he was awarded the title of 'Tiger' after winning the World Wrestling Championship.

CAN AN ORDINARY HUMAN LIFT A 1200kg

Gama threw heavyweight champions of his era like it was nothing more than a tin can on numerous occasions! Unbeaten against numerous champions in a row. Such strength and stamina! He defeated 20 wrestlers in a row!

So why couldn't Gama, the unbeaten behemoth of his time, lift 500kg if today's wrestlers could? GAMA hails from a time when food was extremely nutritious and natural. He used to consume 10 liters of milk every day, as well as one and a half pounds of crushed almond paste mixed with fruit juice in a tonic drink, six desi fowl, a half litre of ghee, six pounds of butter, three buckets of seasonal fruits, two desi muttons, and other things.

These are enough to get him close to being able to lift such a massive weight. If you believe others have lifted such huge artifacts in the past, you may believe GAMA hauled a 1200kg stone that is now housed at the museum.

14

CHAPTER THREE

HIS MYSTERIOUS DEATH

Gama Pehalwan was an 82-year-old legendary wrestler. In this page, you'll learn about his cause of death, religion, and more.

Ghulam Mohammad Baksh Butt was a strongman and Pehalwan i wrestler in British India. On May 22, 1878, he was born and died on May 23, 1960. Rustam-e-Hind and The Great Gama are some of his other names. He was the unquestioned world champion in wrestling in the early twentieth century.

Gama also rose to recognition in 1895, when he competed in a match against Raheem Bakhsh Sultani Wala, the Indian Wrestling Champion at the time. Raheem Bakhsh Sultani Wala was an ethnic Kashmiri wrestler from Gujranwala in Colonial India's Punjab Province (now in Pakistan).

According to multiple accounts, he suffered from a chronic illness in the days preceding up to his death and struggled to pay for the medical treatment he needed. His health was alleged to have deteriorated, and he had previously suffered from asthma and heart problems. He was obliged to sell his medals at the eleventh hour because of his precarious financial circumstances.

GREATEST GAMA

Up until his death, the government provided Gama with property and a monthly stipend, as well as financial support for his medical needs. In order to help him, this was done. At the age of 82, he died in 1960.

Religion and family background of Gama Pehalwan

Ghulam Mohammad Baksh was born in Jabbowal Village, Punjab Province, British India, on May 22, 1878. His ancestors were Kashmiri Muslims who wrestled (now Jabbowal, Kapurthala District, Punjab, India).

In addition, at the age of 10, he competed in a strongman tournament in Jodhpur, which brought him to the notice of the public. He was the youngest competitor in the competition, which included a variety of physically demanding sports including squats.

Due to his youth, the Maharaja of Jodhpur awarded Gama the title of champion. The tournament featured almost 400 wrestlers.

The Maharaja of Datia then taught Gama the skills of the warrior.

Gama Pehalwan, a legendary wrestler, is famous for never losing a match in his 50-year career. He earned the nickname
GREATEST GAMA

"Tiger" as a result of his numerous triumphs, which included the World Heavyweight Championship in 1910 and the World Wrestling Championship in 1927. Gamma resurrected himself as the wrestler Rustam-e-Hind around the turn of the century.

There are even claims that he once faced American martial artist Bruce Lee. Lee became a huge fan of Gama after seeing his training program and nutrition. Gama's exercises were quickly adopted by Lee.

The "cat stretch" and "squat," also known as "baithak" and "deep-knee bend," were two of Lee's favorite workout moves. In the final match of his life, the great wrestler battled Jess Peterson, a Swedish wrestler.

TOUGHEST OPPONNENT

At the age of 17, Gama Pehalwan made headlines when he challenged Raheem Bakhsh Sultani Wala, the 7-foot-tall Indian wrestling champion of the time.

Sultani Wala, a wrestler with a diminutive frame of 5 feet 7 inches, was anticipated to win the battle easily. However, the teenage wrestler gave it his best throughout the contest, which lasted many hours before ending in a draw.

Except for his first opponent, Sultani Wala, Gama had defeated all of India's finest wrestlers by 1910. He changed his

GREATEST GAMA

concentration to the west and sailed to England to compete with wrestlers from the west.

He couldn't enter the tournament right away because of his short stature. But then he issued a challenge: in thirty minutes, he would fight three wrestlers and win all three matches. He was still without a match.

Following that, he issued a challenge to certain heavyweight wrestlers, promising that if he lost, he would pay a prize and return to his homeland. Benjamin Roller was his first Western opponent, who he defeated in 1.40 minutes the first time and 9.10 minutes the second time. He won a berth in the tournament the next day after defeating 12 wrestlers.

He couldn't enter the tournament right away because of his short stature. But then he issued a challenge: in thirty minutes, he would fight three wrestlers and win all three matches. He was still without a match. Following that, he issued a challenge to certain heavyweight wrestlers, promising that if he lost, he would pay a prize and return to his homeland. Benjamin Roller was his first Western opponent, who he defeated in 1.40 minutes the first time and 9.10 minutes the second time. He won a berth in the tournament the next day after defeating 12 wrestlers. Gama

GREATEST GAMA

competed against Stanislaus Zbyszko, regarded as one of the best wrestlers of all time.

Zbyszko was brought down by the renowned wrestler during their encounter in 1910 and remained there for the next two hours. The audience erupted when Zbyszko was on the defensive and managed a draw. Zbyszko failed not show up for their second face-off, so Gama was declared the winner.

He faced Sultani Wala again later in his career, and this time he won the battle and the Rustam-e-Hind championship. Sultani Wala was always regarded as Gama's most formidable adversary. The Great Gama used to put in a lot of effort in the gym. He used to wrestle 40 wrestlers per day, followed by 5,000 squats and 3,000 push-ups.

His diet was equally bizarre; he drank four gallons of milk every day, along with one and a half pounds of crushed almond paste made by combining various fruit liquids.

GREATEST GAMA

GAMAS FAMILY
Aslam Pahalwan

On January 15, 1927, the Great Gama Pehalwan and one of his wives, Imam Baksh Pahalwan, gave birth to Aslam Pahalwan, a Pakistani wrestler.

In so many ways, Aslam resembled his father. As far back as 1968, he was the World Heavyweight Champion and ranked No. 9 in the world. "The Wrestling King" was his other moniker.

He was known as the All India Champion throughout Europe and America.

Aslam traveled the United Kingdom, taking on opponents in high-profile venues such as the North, Midlands, and Scotland, and defeating Canadian Champion George Gordienko along the way.

Aslam received the Government of Pakistan's Pride of Performance Award in 1967.

Orig Williams, a British wrestling promoter, was his manager at the time, while Christopher Whelan, another British promoter, was his sponsor.

In the 1970s, Aslam stepped away from the ring. He died in Pakistan in 1989, at the age of 61, and was succeeded as world champion by his son Jhara Pahalwan.

Aslam Pahalwan started off as a student of Hamida Pahalwan and India's Great Gama. He started wrestling in the 1940s. He used to workout three times a day, mostly doing Pahalwani exercises like dands, Indian-style pushups, baithaks, and squats in the local dialect. He also engaged in a variety of other exercises to increase his strength, endurance, and flexibility.

To maintain his body weight after a strenuous workout, he ate a nutritious, high-calorie diet. He is said to have consumed an entire goat in one sitting.

He began his career competing in events conducted around India, mainly in Punjab. In Amritsar, he won his first wrestling match in ninety seconds against Indian Bala Pahalwan.

He beat Niranjan Singh in less than two minutes at Patiala. Prior to independence, the Maharaja of Patiala held an annual wrestling tournament in his princely domain during the Islamic month of Moharram. In the finals of one of these tournaments, Aslam defeated Puran Singh.

GREATEST GAMA

Aslam Pahalwan gave up wrestling in the early 1970s. On January 7, 1989, he died at the age of 61 in Pakistan. His son Jhara Pahalwan was a champion wrestler as well.

Gamas Wives

Gama Pehalwan has two wives. His wives were Wazeer Begum and another lady. In addition to their names, there is no information about his spouses. They do, however, appear to have stuck by Gama through thick and thin.

Gama Pehalwan has five daughters and five sons. Nawaz Sharif's granddaughter Kalsoom Nawaz is his wife, while Jhara Pehalwan is married to Kalsoom's sister Saira Bano, who is Gama's granddaughter.

Gama Pehalwan was born on May 22, 1878, in Jabbowal Village, Punjab Province, British India, to a Kashmiri Muslim wrestling family (now Jabbowal, Kapurthala District, Punjab, India). According to historians, the Bakshs were originally Kashmiri Hindus (Bhat) who converted to Islam during Muslim rule in Kashmir.

GREATEST GAMA

CONCLUSION

This is an unofficial story of indias greatest wrestler gathered from multiple trusted sources.

Gama had great strength which very few people have.

This is because of his bizarre but natural foods he ate from chicken to liters milk everyday shows how strong and healthy we can become.

But today, we eat more of processed foods which are in now way good for us.

The story of gada should inspire us.